L
DIALECT

A selection of words and anecdotes
from around Devon

by
Ellen Fernau

BRADWELL
BOOKS

Published by Bradwell Books
9 Orgreave Close Sheffield S13 9NP
Email: books@bradwellbooks.co.uk

© Ellen Fernau

British Library Cataloguing in Publication Data:
a catalogue record for this book is available from the
British Library.

1st Edition

ISBN: 9781909914001

Print: Gomer Press, Llandysul, Ceredigion SA44 4JL

Artwork and design by: Andrew Caffrey

Photograph Credits:
Unless otherwise stated, all photographs
courtesy of the Totness Image Bank

DEVON DIALECT

by Ellen Fernau

ACKNOWLEDGEMENTS

The entire process of writing this book has been made easier by a supportive cast, in this case led by my husband Tim who kindly chose not to notice as my notes and queries spread all over the house, and the ever growing (and kicking) bump, who held on until the work was complete. Chris Gilbert from Bradwell Books was prepared to put a great deal of faith in me from the outset, for which I am grateful to both him and my sister Louise whose work on the Sussex and Norfolk dialect books blazed a trail that I just needed to follow. Her work, as ever, is exemplary. Thanks also to the Totnes Image Bank, who were extremely helpful with the images used throughout the book. Finally, to the rest of the family: don't think you went unnoticed. My thanks to you all.

DEDICATION

To **Martin Burdick**, who remains unknown to me but whose collection of books on Devon, which found their way to me via to a second hand book shop in Tewkesbury, was invaluable.

Introduction

The English language is now spoken by over 300 million people as a first language with many more using English as a second language, making one in five people across the globe a competent English speaker.

Within our own coastline, there are countless variants of dialect and diversions away from what might be called the Queen's English. Some have wandered far from the textbooks, with Sir Francis Drake (who himself hailed from Devon) having to appoint a translator to communicate at the court of Elizabeth I.

Devon has a unique set of vocal traditions, many developed because of quirks of geography and others from a complex social demography. Many efforts have been made to record the language traditions of the area and to identify the sources of some of the words that are, or used to be, in common use. This book merely touches the surface.

The first part of this book is an A-Z of words and phrases particular to Devon, with their current or historic meanings and some examples of how they may once have been used. The second part is a collection of anecdotes, stories, rhymes and curiosities, all arranged by theme.

The anecdotes may be long or short, complicated or simple, but all contain genuine examples of Devonshire dialect as recorded by historians and collectors over the years.

It is also worth noting that language is constantly evolving and while some of the words noted in this book may not be familiar to current Devonians (although I'd suggest many are gems worth bringing back), new ones will always be developing. I can only hope this book is as much fun to read as it was to research and write.

Ellen Fernau

A

A-long – slanting or at an angle

A-veered – afraid

Addle-headed – thickheaded

Agging – provoking or egging on, possibly nagging

Agin – against

Agone – in the past, as in:

'Twas zome time agone her went up tu gert ouze.'

Aigs - eggs

Aright moi luvver – a phrase, popularised and often in comic use by the media, used as a general greeting. Used across the southwest.

Allernbatch – a big spot or boil

Angle-twitch – the earthworm

Ant – I am not

Appen – perhaps or let's see

Appledrane – a wasp

Apurt – sullen or dogged as in:

'Her's a gone off apurt.'

Arnt – I am not

Arter – after

Avore – before

Ax – ask

Axen – ashes

Axwaddler / axicaddle – a dealer in ashes which used

to be a key ingredient in the making of alkalies for soaps. Ashes from coal or wood fires had to be carefully distinguished and the axwaddlers would have been well known travelling businessmen in rural communities.

B

Baa-lamb – a nursery term for a lamb

Baccy – tobacco for smoking

Bachelor's buttons – the flowers of the common burdock

Baggage – a saucy wench

Bagger – a scarecrow. A pony could be rated by several characteristics, as noted in this rhyme:

He can car' whisky
Can zmul a pixy
An'wud'n cocky to a gaily bagger.

Baint – isn't

Ballyrag – to scold or reprimand

Bamby – by and by

Banging – large or great

Banging-gert – very large indeed, as in:

'I've just a-zeed a banging-gert otter down tha river.'

Barbs – sticks

Barnstaple Fair Pears – a delicious sweet dessert that is attributed to the farmers who delivered pears to Barnstaple market. They were simmered in scrumpy until tender and sold as a sweet.

Barthless – without a house, possibly from the nautical
term 'berth'

Be – commonly used in the present tense, as in:

'I be not a varmer.'

Beant – am not

Belike – perhaps

Bewhivered – bewildered or frightened

Bettermot – somewhat superior or better

Billers – cow parsnip

Bladders - blister

Blaijed – obliged

Blake – to burst with laughter or cry out until
you are out of breath

Blenky / blunk / blenked – to snow lightly, or sparks
and ashes that may fly out of the fire

Blid - blood

Bloody warrior – the wallflower

Blooth – a blossom or flower

Boit – a meal or refreshment

Boneshave – backache or sciatica

Boozy / bosky – tipsy or a bit drunk

Bowerly – an attractive lady, in good health

Bozzam / bozzam-chucked – having a redness
in the cheeks

Braggoijj – speckled

Brath – broth, which may not always be welcome, as a sickly schoolboy once said:

'Brath! Whot brath again! Why twas brath yesterday,
brath tha day avore, brath tiday and mayhap
'tweel be brath again tu-morrar!'

Brimmels – brambles

Brimbly – full of brambles

Briss – rubbish or dust

Buldering – sweltering, as in a hot, muggy day

Bulhaggle – a scarecrow

Bullins – wild plums

Butt – dung cart or bee hive

Butter-and-eggs – a particular type of daffodil

Buttons – sheeps dung

C

Cab – sticky, or cold and damp, as in:

'That washing is all of a cab.'

Canker – poisonous fungus

Casar – sieve for winnowing corn

Cass'n / cassn't – I can't or can't you, depending on the inflection

Cathandid – clumsy

Cats-tails – the catkins of the hazelnut tree

Cauch – mess or disgusting mixture

Caw! – an exclamation of surprise

Chaps – cheeks

Charewoman / chewrer - someone who helps the servants with difficult or less attractive tasks

Cheek-by-jowl – packed in close together

Cheel – child

Chell – I shall

Chet – a kitten

Chilbladders – chilblains

Chimley – a chimney

Chit – a troublesome or cheeky child

Chockiling – the cackling of a disturbed hen or a person giving a scolding

Clam / clapper– something to help with the crossing of a stream, like a stick to clamber along, if there is no bridge to use

Cleg – a horsefly

Cleves – cliffs

Clider – the herb goosegrass

Clinkers – the ashes left in a smiths forge or a fireplace

Clipper – a knock

Clodhopper – a country bumpkin, not usually meant as a compliment

Clopping – lame or limping

Clotted cream – a Devonshire speciality, made by baking double cream at a low heat for two to three hours and

scooping off the thick layer and crust on the top.
The watery residue is discarded.

Clovel – the beam across a mantelpiece

Clume – crockery

Clummersome – dirty or inappropriate

Clunk – to swallow

Clutter – rushed or haphazard

Cob – mud mixed with straw, used in wall building

Cockleert – daybreak

Codger – an old man. In the past this may not have been meant fondly, but use has softened in recent times.

Coltee – to be as playful as a young colt

Combe – a hollow between two hills

Condiddle – to hide away secretly

Conkabell – an icicle

Copper finch – a chaffinch

Cooche-handed – left handed

Corniwillin – a lapwing

Cotton – to beat soundly

Courtlage – the yard of a house

Cow-flop / flop-dock – the foxglove

Craytures – creatures

Crewdling – an unattractive, cold or disagreeable person

Crim – a small part, or a bit as in:
  'Stay a crim.' or 'Not worth a crim.'

Croping – stingy

Crookers – horns

Crowd / crowder– to fiddle or play the violin, a fiddler

Crowdy – a violin

Crub / crubby – the crust of the bread or dry, stale bread

Cruel – very or extremely

Cryamaces – abbreviation of Christ have mercy, all as one word

Cuddie – the wren

Culver – the woodpigeon

Curry – to thrash or whack, as in:

> *'I'll curry your hide.'*

Cursemas – Christmas

> *Vather stawl the passen's sheep,*
> *A murry Cursemas us'll keep,*
> *Vur us chell 'ave boath vitals an' drink,*
> *But dawnt zay nort about et.*

Cuz - because

D

Dab – an insignificant person, or a light blow

Daggle – to run like a young child

Dairus – bold

Dang'it – an exclamation of dismay, derived from dash it

Daps – likeness, as in he was the daps of someone, or exact likeness

Dark – blind, for instance someone may be dark in one eye

Darter – daughter

Dashel – thistle

Dawcock – a silly chap

Deef – rotten or corrupt

Dere – to hurry along, particularly a child

Devonshire flats – sweet biscuits traditionally made with Devonshire clotted cream

Devonshire split – a small, sweet bread roll, served with cream and jam as a Devonshire speciality

Devonshire squab pie – a savoury pie, topped with shortcrust pastry, which confusingly is traditionally not made with squab (young pigeons) but mutton or lamb. Put together in layers with apples and spices, it has a number of variants across the south west, but the Devonshire custom is to serve it with clotted cream.

Dide – died

Dildrams – an unlikely story

Dimmet – dusk or evening twilight

Dinder – thunder

Dirsh – thrush

Diss'n – don't you

Doattee – to nod the head as you are falling asleep

Dood – done

Dreckly – directly, as in:

    'I'll be there dreckly.'

Dree – three

Drang / drangway– a narrow lane or passage

Drenking – a meal taken in the afternoon, originally by labourers working the fields. Notably, it has nothing to do with the cider allowance which could be taken at any time of day.

Drippence – threepence

Drizzle – an unrelenting fine rain

Drumble-drain – a bumble bee

Dyver'd – faded

E

Eart one, eart t'other – now one and then the other

Ees – yes

Eese – his

Eet – yet

Emmet – an ant

Enew – enough

Errish – a stubble field

Evet – a small lizard or newt

Exeter pudding – a baked pudding, with layers of sponge, raisins, custard and fruit

F

F / V – these letters are commonly interchangeable or approximated with something inbetween

Fadge – fare, as in:

'How d'ye fadge?'

Figs – raisins, hence figgy pudding is a raisin pudding in Devonshire. Also, confusingly, is plum pudding, which usually contains no plums.

Fitty – clever

Flabberghasted – confounded or amazed

Flicketts – flushed or blushing

Flosh – to spill

Fozy – a choice mouthful or morsel

Fump – whole, as in:

'He told me the fump of the story.'

Furtig – fatigue

Fussocky – to bustle about and fuss

Fust – first

Fusti-luggs – a larger or big boned person

Fy! – an expression of surprise or disapproval

G

Gafter – an old man

Galliment – a scarecrow or birdscarer

Gally – to scare

Gammerell – the calf or lower leg

Gammet – fun or merriment

Ganmer – an old lady

Gapesnest – a strange sight, or fit only for staring at

Gawkim – stupid fellow

Giglet – an exuberant youth

Giglet fair – the annual town fair, as in Okehampton Giglet Fair. These were often lively affairs and offered the opportunity for entertainment, trading goods, hiring new staff and, legend has it, the buying and selling of wives.

Girt / gert / gurt – large or big

Girtly – greatly

Gladdie – the yellow hammer

Glam – an injury, wound or sore

Glidder / a-glidder – slippery or sliding

Glowing – staring

Glowering – quarrelsome

Glumping – sullen or sulky

Go – often interchangeable for gone, as in:
   'He be a-go fishing.'

Goose-chickens – the catkins of the willow

Gorbelly – having a large paunch or stomach

Granfer – grandfather

Gray – badger

Grizzledemundy – a cheerful person, possibly excessively so

Grockle – a modern term for a tourist or summer visitor, adapted from broader west country slang for travellers

Gullet – the arch of a bridge

Gumption – energy and determination, with an early meaning of common sense

Gwain – going

H

Haggage – a slattern, or lady of ill repute

Haid – head

Half-baked – stupid or slow-witted, or as the locals might describe it:

> *'He wuz putt in wi' the braid an took out wi' the cakes.'*

Halzening – predicting the worst that could happen or generally wishing evil

Ham – a water meadow or pasture, derived from the saxon word ham for farm

Hantick – mad or unstable

Hap – chance

Hapmy – halfpenny

Hare – she. Her and she can be used interchangeably.

Hatchet-faced – a person with a sharp face or with deep lines

Hay-maidens – ground ivy

Heave-up – a commotion or disturbance

Hedgeboar – hedgehog

Heft – the weight of something

Hewstring – coughing and wheezing

Hobbyhorse – to romp or play boisterously, or a tomboy. See also the custom of Hunting for the Earl of Rone.

Hoop – a bullfinch

Hornywink – lapwing

Horry – mouldy

Hotch – to drive cattle

Houdery – looking like rain or overcast

Hulking – lubberly or gangly

Humman / umman – a woman or women

Hunch – a large portion of food

Hurtleberry – the bilberry plant, or bilberries

Huzzy – a case for a needle and thread

I

Ize – I am

J

Jags – rags, as in to dress in rags

Jasper – wasp

Janner – now used as a reference for the people of Plymouth, perhaps originally from Jan, the Devon form of John. Likely a word that used to refer to people who made their living from the sea in the Plymouth area.

Jit – a push or sharp slap

Jonic – truthful or honest

Juggy-mire – a swamp or bog

Junket – a milk based pudding, and Devonshire delicacy. Recipes vary throughout the county, but all are based on sweetened milk, mixed with rennet and left to set. You could add rum, brandy, sherry or fruit, or simply put cream on top. It has been noted that 'The marriage of cream with junket is, perhaps, one of the most blissful of unions.'

K

Kep – a cap

Kerp – to crow about something, particularly to the detriment of someone else

Keslings – wild plums

Kickhammer – someone who stammers

Kicking – fashionable or well dressed

Kickshaws – new inventions or foreign imports

Kindiddled – enticed

Kiss'n – can't

L

Lablolly – a silly person

Lace – to beat, for instance with a stick

Lary – empty

Law – an exclamation as in:
    'Oh law!'

Leastwise – at least

Lendy – bendy or flexible

Lidden – a tale or yarn

Limperskrimp – wild celery

Linhay – an outbuilding or barn which may be derelict

Locks-and-keys – the seed pods of the ash and sycamore

Lobby – sweet and sticky

Loblolly-boy – errand boy

Long-cripple – the viper or adder

Lookeedeezee – look do you see, all pronounced as one word

Lunnen – London

M

Make-wise – to pretend, or make out that something is true

Malls – the measles

Mang – mix

Maunder – to grumble or mumble to yourself

Mazzard – a Devonshire strain of small black cherry

Meade – meadow

Mean – to demonstrate with your hands,
to indicate without speaking

Meech – to play truant

Meets – to even up, as in:

> *'I'll be meets with 'im eventually.'*

Mengy – a minnow

Merzuk – myself

Methiglin – local wine made from honey

Mickled – feeling the cold, frozen or numb

Merchivus – mischievous

Moat – the stump or roots of a tree

Moil – a mule

Mommet – a scarecrow

Moor – an expanse of wild countryside, hence Exmoor and Dartmoor

Mortal – very

Mow – meadow or field

Mucks – mud

Mummers – groups of actors who travel around local pubs, performing traditional plays

N

Naddling – nodding

Nare – never

Nawse – nose

Neart – night

Niff / take niffy – to take offence or get in a huff

Niver-the-near – useless or to no purpose

Nort – nought or nothing

Nummet – lunch

Nuthin – nothing

O

O'at – of that

Opp – open, as in:

'It's already opp.'

Ort – anything

Oss – horse

Over-get – to overtake or pass by

Owets – oats

P

Paddle – to partake of a little liquor

Pakin – strolling

Pangers – panniers, which when used poetically, gives us:

He'th a-got no more manners

Than a 'oss with a pair o'pangers

Parfit – perfect

Passon – parson

Peer – pair

Pickle – condition, as in:

'Well, crimminy, yer's a go! Yu be in a defful pickle!'

Pigsloose – a pigsty
Pillamy / pilm – dust
Pillum – dirt
Pilth – fluff
Pindy – musty
Pinikin – delicate
Pip / take the pip – to take something amiss
or miss the joke
Pister – a word most commonly used alongside 'whister'
to imply secrets being whispered, for instance children
may be whistering and pistering between themselves
Pixy / picksey – an elf or sprite
Pixey-led – being pixey led is to experience something
uncanny or unnerving, which may occur either before one
or two glasses of scrumpy, or after. The bleak character of
the moors led even well seasoned travellers to lose their
way under some circumstances, and being pixey led was
often the given cause
Pixy-puff – the puffball
Pixy-rings – rings of greener grass commonly found in
fields and gardens
Pixy-stool – a toadstool
Planching – a wooden floor
Prist – priest
Proper job – a phrase popularised by the media
meaning something done well or a general expression of

satisfaction. Used across the south west.

Pucksey – wet muddy ground

Pugging end – the gable end

Punkel – punctual

Purty – pretty

Q

Quelstring – hot and sultry weather

Querk – to grunt or moan in pain

R

Rare-mouse – a bat

Rawse – rose

Reeping – trailing in the dirt

Rist – rust

Rittling – wheezing

Rory-tory – showy or colourful

Round-shaving – a lecture or reprimand

Ruckee – to stoop down low

S

S / Z – these letters are commonly interchangeable or approximated with something inbetween

Sarment – sermon

Sartin – certain

Scatt – a shower of rain, as used in a proverb in the village on Kenton:

'When Halldown has a hat, let Kenton beware of a scatt.'

Here a hat presumably indicates a covering of cloud.

Scrawf – to refuse

Scrumpy – Devonshire's own recipe for cider, made from the apples that fall from the trees. Devon has an incredibly wide range of apple varieties, many particularly suitable for cider making.

Scud – a scab

Scute – a reward

Shab off – to sneak away or skulk into retreat

Shear-a-muze – a bat

Sheeps-eyes – favourable glances

Shord – a gap in the hedge

Siss – a larger lady

Skiddik – a thing

Skittering – slight or slim, flyaway

Slock / slockster – to pilfer / pilferer

Sloudring – clumsy or inept

Smitch – to blacken with soot or smoke

Soger – soldier

Spalliard – a sparrow

Spare – slow

Spray – chapped or rough skin

Spuddle / spuddler – to stir or rake about, or someone who is trying to stir up trouble

Steeved – stiffened with cold

Stewer – dust

Stickle – steep, perhaps like a stickle path

Stogged – mired in mud or clay

Stram – to hear or make a loud and sudden noise

Strat in the chops – a blow to the face

Stude – stood

Suffing – sobbing

T

Tack – to strike with the flat of the hand and by extension tack hands, meaning to clap hands together

Take on / to take by – to feel sad or be affected by a sad event

Tallet – a hay-loft

Tatties – potatoes, although some efforts have been made to update this shortening. A lad who took work in the midlands returned home to Devonshire to hear his father talk about '*dayzays in tha tatties*'. He implored his father: '*Fayther, pleeze toe remember the 'per'. Say pertatties. Tis fery fulgar to say tatties*'.

Tidd'n – it isn't

Tiffles – down flying in the air, as you might find when making the bed

Tiz – It is. e.g. Yer tiz me dear.

Ted / tet – to be ordered or instructed to do something, or bound by obligation, as in:

   '*I ted go home at dimmet.*'

Thumping – great or huge

Thunder-bolt – the scarlet poppy, as found in cornfields

Tizzick – a cold on the chest

Tor – a mound or steep hill, as in Torbay

Tottle – to toddle or walk unsteadily as a child

Troant – a lazy loiterer

Try – faring, as in:

   '*How do you try?*'

Tummil'd – tumbled

Tweedle – to twist

U

Ull – will

Upsetting – a christening feast or gathering of gossips, for instance after a wedding or funeral.

Up-country – anywhere north of Devon, as in:

   '*I used to live in Devon but now I have moved up-country.*'

Upsides – to be even with someone or a good match

Urch – rich

Urn – run

Us'd – we had

Uv – of

V

V / F – these letters are commonly interchangeable or approximated with something inbetween

Vady – damp or foggy

Vair – fair

Vall – fall, as in: *'Me and my old man'th valled out.'*

Vantysheeny – showy

Varm – farm

Veaking – fretful or peevish

Vitty – decent, handsome or generally well

Vokes – folks or people

Vont – the font in a church

Vor – for

Vorrad – forward

Vramp-shapen – distorted or misshapen

Vrom – from

Vule – fool

Vun – fun as in: *'An then the vun began…'*

Vussled – hurried

Vustling – fussing

W

Wambling – an upset or loud stomach, or waving and rolling about

Wan – one

Wangery – tired or flabby

Want – a mole

Wapper-hy'd – sleepy or tired

Warre and warre – worse and worse

Washamouth – a blab or tale teller

Washdish – a wagtail

Wayout – without

Wee-wow – waving about this way and that

Well to pass – doing well, or thriving

Whacker – great

Wheal – mine

Whistercluster – a blow under the ear

Windle – the robin

Wisterpoop – a knock

White-pot – a pudding made in Devon, containing flour, milk and eggs with raisins and spices, like a custard pudding

Woodquist – woodpigeon

Worrit – worried

Wrecker – people who deliberately attracted ships to their doom on to the rugged Devon coastline, with the intention of plundering the cargo. In this case, legend may well be just that, with no basis in historical fact.

Wuss – worse

Y

Yavill – a common or local heath
Yer – here
Yewshil – usual
Yewbrimmel – a local name for the wild dog-rose
Yu'm / yourn – you are
Yummers – embers of a fire

Z

Z / S – these letters are commonly interchangeable or approximated with something inbetween
Zaw – saw
Zawl – soul, as in: *'Caw! Bless my zawl!'*
Zee – see
Zes – says
Zider – cider, which can bring out the poet in anyone:

I likes zider and zider likes me,
I'll drink zider as long as I can zee.
I likes zider and zider likes I,
An' I'll drink zider till I do die.

Zin – the sun or a son
Zogging – a snooze or dozing
Zmacks – kisses
Zoxverswopped – ill-natured or crabby
Zummer – summer

Pronunciation and Usage

View from Bickleigh Church Tower

In 1907 The Bishop of Exeter, in his presidential address to the Devonshire Association, said *"genuine dialect is as true and undefiled a tongue as the purest speech of Chaucer and Milton."* He later voiced his serious concerns that the local language was being lost, with only decades left before it was so dilute as to be unrecognisable.

His worries would turn out to be well founded. Across the country, the nuances that make regional language so unique are being lost to time. This may be because we now travel so widely, or because we consciously err on the side of a national 'standardised' language in order to blend in or disguise our regional roots.

In whatever case, looking backwards, the language of the south-west has certainly developed differently from the rest of the country. Along with the majority of what is now England and Wales, the area was originally populated by the Britton tribe. The language that they established had Celtic origins and was known as Brittonic.

When the Romans came, they didn't extend their reach much beyond Exeter with archaeological remains being thinly spread beyond the end of their most westerly major road, Fosse Way. When they finally left in around 410AD, they left Britain open to the Saxons, who brought their own Germanic tongue.

Once again, although the Anglo-Saxons were successful in taking the territories to the east, the Britons held on to key strongholds in the south-west, Wales, parts of Cumbria and Galloway. In these areas the language was left to evolve in unique ways and today there are strong movements to preserve and record the words and phrases that came to be.

While each area of Devon has its own character, some general rules can be applied to the region's dialect as a whole. There is a common trend of putting an extra vowel into place names which did not originally contain them: for instance it would not have been uncommon to hear locals refer to Dartmoor as *Dart-i-moor*. In some cases the names have stuck, in cases like Widdecombe, Wollacombe, Westaway and Ellacott.

Likewise, an *f* is commonly replaced by a *v*, and vice versa (however tempting it may be to say *fice fersa*). This gives such words as *vor* (four), *vorth* (fourth) and *vair* (fair). Just as interchangeable are the *z* and *s*, giving *zay* (say) and *zo* (so). You will also find yourself pronouncing the 'r' in many words with far greater distinction in Devon than you might elsewhere, for instance farm may be pronounced more along the lines of *'varr'um'*.

In some areas, unique events have conspired to create local variants. In the small hamlet of Bucks Mill on the north Devon coast, there is a chance that some Spanish connections have embedded themselves in the local speech patterns. A ship from the Spanish Armada was said to have been wrecked nearby and a few members of the crew washed ashore. Rescued by locals, and in the isolation of the hamlet, the crew members evaded capture by English troops and integrated into the local community, bringing with them their own colloquialsims.

Devon also has a wide variety of extreme terrains, with the moors offering as much to the local character as the coastline. The moors are huge, isolated expanses of land. The farming communities that maintain a toehold there specialise mainly in animal husbandry, but only the toughest breeds of sheep, pony and indeed farmer can remain on the upper moorlands in the winter.

The inaccessibility of many areas is compounded by the general acceptance that in Devon, the roads are good, bad, or entirely non-existent. In days gone by, if you left the main highways you took your chances and were generally advised to avoid anything that looked like it might be a shortcut. You were just as likely to find yourself on a track full of *'pucksey holes'* in which you, your horse or vehicle could get *'stogged up'* for hours. On the moors this is compounded by the many winding bridle paths and tracks. In the past they may have been useful for concealing the smugglers carrying contraband to one of the many caves and caverns they used as hideouts: to today's tourists they offer ample opportunity to get lost. The Devonshire boundary also has a particular claim to fame. Devon is the only county in the UK which has two entirely distinct coastlines, unconnected to each other. Both have a wealth of small seafaring communities, now considered picture-postcard beautiful and magnets for tourists, but in the past providing some critical income to the region. The crafts and industry associated with the sea are also embedded in the local folklore, with many local legends centring on sailors, ships and the fishing trade.

Devon is a diverse county and many different adaptations of the dialect have developed within it making a single record very difficult to produce. There are also more practical concerns. The Hartland Forum, which is collating many examples of local history, tells the story of the Rev Fred Pennington who set about a project to record some of his parishioners speaking, capturing both their memories as well as their speech patterns. He set himself up with a reel-to-reel tape recorder and microphone, but when he started the conversation he found his subjects reverting to their best Queen's English. When asked why, one participant said:

"Tis the machine Fred, tin't viddy
wi such a thing bout e hummin."

Traditions and Customs

Milk for clotted cream

The south-west of Britain has a plethora of traditions and folklore, owing much to its remote geography and historical separation from the rest of the country. There are even cultural divisions within its own boundaries, with one of the most fiercely contested being the correct serving of the ever popular cream tea.

In a Devonshire tea, cream tops the split scone first, followed by spoonful of jam. A Cornish cream tea should only ever be served with jam spread first on the two slices of scone, which is only then topped with a dollop of clotted cream. Each area vehemently defends the accuracy of their tradition.

And any investigation into Devonshire's culinary delights should go no further without some mention of cider, or scrumpy. Each farmer once put the greatest store by their own particular recipe for making the brew, usually comprising a blend of the unique mix of apples they grew on their own farm. Passing travellers might find the local farmers most hospitable with their wares:

"Tez mortel 'ot tuday zit; wantee plaize tu come inside an' 'a drap of zyder? Ours be a prime zort, I zuree."

Cider apple harvest

Of course pubs were also likely to trade on the quality of the local drink, with one pub sign being noted as saying:

Yer in zyder tu cheer
And fery gude beer
And ef yu want a trayte
There be rabbits tu ayte.

This is typical of the kind of straightforward advice you are likely to get from a local. Although Devonshire folk will give you a hearty welcome, they do not have a reputation for particular humour or wit.

As J. HENRY HARRIS noted in '*My Devonshire Book*':

"Devonshire humour is homely, and if you are in too much of a hurry you may miss it altogether. Some persons who have scampered through the towns and villages speak of the inhabitants as stolid, and stupid and morose because they don't make any effort to show their bright side at a moment's notice. Quick witted they are not, but they accommodate their pace to their wit and are apt to turn matters over and over and then sleep on them before acting.

Devon folk do not cut you short with something brilliant, like an Irishman, for example, and must have their own way. First of all they make an atmosphere and fill in the details, and then, all unconsciously, something is said which gives a humorous turn to the narrative."

There is certainly a compliment in there somewhere, although you may need to read through twice to find it. Rest assured that Harris' book as a whole leaves the reader in no doubt that he had a great love for the county and its folk. Yet he was not alone in noting the intellectual challenges some locals face. In Charles Kingsley's *'Westward Ho!'* (which has the distinction of lending its name to a village, making it the only one in the country to have an exclamation mark in its name), the main character, Amyas Leigh, is introduced to the reader in less than favourable terms:

> *"He held that the swallows slept all the winter at the bottom of the horse-pond; talked, like Raleigh, Grenville, and other low persons, with a broad Devonshire accent; and was in many other respects so very ignorant a youth, that any pert monitor in a national school might have had a hearty laugh at him."*

The connection between a west country accent and rural simplicity has long been played up in literature and the media. As often as not, if a character speaks with a Devonshire burr it is an indicator that they may be slightly innocent or un-worldly-wise, for instance in the case of Hagrid in the Harry Potter films, or the portrayals of the hobbits Merry and Pippin in The Lord of the Rings.

The changing trends of the times were noted in the first verses of one song, aptly called *'The Last of the Singers'*:

> *I reckon the days is departed*
> *When folk 'ud listen to me,*

And I feels like as one broken-hearted,
A-thinking o' what used to be
And I don't know as much be amended,
Than was in them merry old Times
When, wi' pipes and good old ale, folks attended,
To me and my purty ol' rhymes.

'Tis true, I be cruel asthmatic
I've lost every tooth I' my head;
And my limbs be that crim'd wi'rheumatic
D'rsay I were better in bed.
Oh my! All the world be for reading
Newspapers, and books and what not;
Sure – 'tis only conceitedness breeding,
And the old singing man is forgot.

Cott Inn

These changes should not always be taken as a weakness though, as Devonshire folk are also known for being determined and resourceful. It is worth remembering that some of the most famous explorers in history have come from Devon, including Captain Robert Scott of the Antarctic and Sir Francis Drake. Little wonder, when so much of the rugged and exposed Devonshire countryside and coastline warrants exploration. There are hidden coves, high moorlands and deep caves, all offering the Devonshire locals a perfect training ground for the terrains they could find overseas.

But travel does not take away from a fierce local pride. One local in Ivybridge was deeply troubled when structural engineers condemned the ivy on the bridge, that may well have given the town its name, as likely to cause long term damage and in need of removal. The work complete, the chap was heard to say:

"You's a bucket o' sut; take and chuck un auver that new mortar o' yurs; us don't want our old bridge looking so white and naked as that."

However not all of the local character is in the people, landscape, or bricks and mortar. Pixies are an enduring legend in both Devon and Cornwall. Thought to be small, generally benign, and usually mischievous, many stories tell of the occasions when people and these little sprites cross paths. One has taken root to such an extent that an annual event still takes place to commemorate its significance. In Ottery St Mary the local pixie community were not keen on the increasing popularity of Christianity, which encouraged its followers to deny that they even existed. The building of a church was the final straw, as it is well known in the area that pixies hate the sound of church bells.

Although the little sprites waged a tireless campaign, the bells were eventually installed and the pixies fled to live in exile in a cave at Pixie's Parlour on the banks of the river Otter. They tried to have the final word, however, by sneaking back into the town and capturing the bell ringers. Although the ringers escaped, the pixie ambush is re-enacted every year by the local Cub, Scout and Brownie groups in celebration of the final liberation of the town from its miniature mischief makers. The addition of a fete now offers a beer tent to the beleaguered bell ringers, as well as fireworks for today's marauding pixie hoard. In another tale, Jimmy Townsend lived happily on the moor, with his sister Grace. All would have been well, except for his insistence that his real sister had been stolen away as an infant by the *'pisgies'* and a sprite left in her place. He insisted: *"Her wasn' a twelve-month old avor her was stole away, an' a pisgie put in her cradle in her place. I knaw 'tis so, vor her grawed up sich a cross tempered little mortal as you ever zeed, an' whoever's got anything to do wi' her will sure to come to some harm."*

The supernatural plays a great part in the folklore of the south-west and many strange customs have been noted in Devon over the years. When asked why he thrust his spoon through the end of the shell of his eaten boiled egg, one Devonian said: *"Tu keep they baggering witches vrom agwaine to zay in an egg-boat."* Put into a rhyme, the custom is made clearer:

You must break the shell to bits, for fear
The witches should make it a boat, my dear;
For over the sea, away from home
Far by night the witches roam.

Harvest group

44

Many traditions have not stood the test of time so well, although they are well recorded. At harvest-time, many communities commemorated the cutting of the last sheaf of corn with a variant of a custom commonly referred to as '*Crying the Neck*'. The best ears of corn were selected and woven into a corn dolly, which was then paraded in various forms to hollers of:

We-ha-neck! We-ha neck!
Well-a-cut! Well-a-cut!
Well-a-bound! Well-a-bound!
Well a zot upon tha ground!
We-ha-neck! We-ha-neck!
Wurrah, wurrah, wurrah!

Cider drinkers

It was an occasion for letting off steam after a season of hard work and the ensuing celebrations, certainly accompanied by cider, were well earned.

Shrove Tuesday was welcomed with just as much enthusiasm by many. The impending feast before the beginning of Lent was taken as an opportunity for mischief making, and in Devon the night before Shrove Tuesday became known as Dappy-door night. Children would visit the various houses in the parish in the hope of being given flour, butter or eggs to contribute to the pancake day feast.

In Ilfracombe, however, the children were just as likely to knock on the door and run away, or even tie the door closed. In Hartland, the following rhyme marks the occasion:

Flish, flash; flish, flash;
Watter, watter, ling.
Hev ee any pancakes?
Plaize vor let us in.
Hev ee any best beer?
Hev ee any small?
Plaize vor gie us zomthin'
Or nothin' at all.

One custom that may have less to do with religion and more to do with a degree of public humiliation is Honiton's Hot Pennies Day.

Originally linked to the Honiton Fair, which has its roots as far back as the 13th century, in this tradition hot pennies were thrown from pub windows to children in the streets below, to the amusement of onlookers who watched while the children proceeded to burn their fingers while picking the pennies up. The exact purpose of this custom seems to be lost in time, but needless to say that today's version only involves warm rather than scalding coins.

Honiton Fair has one or two other curious customs, including an opening ceremony that culminates in the hoisting of a golden glove and a loud proclamation from the town crier that *"The Glove is up! The Fair is begun! No man shall be arrested!"*

Legend has it that the Fair was an occasion when people could settle old scores in any way they saw fit, without fear of arrest.

Brent fair

One final custom amongst the many that can be found alive and thriving in the Devonshire villages, is the Hunting of the Earl of Rone which is commemorated each year in Coombe Martin. Although the history of the occasion doesn't bear much scrutiny, it was revived in 1974 and has now become a key event in the local calendar. Legend has it that the Earl of Tyrone survived a shipwreck and hid in the woods above Coombe Martin. Having existed solely on a small supply of ship's biscuits that he had managed to salvage, he was eventually found and taken into custody by a party of Grenadiers. The local celebrations add extra layers of colour to the tale. Each year, a party of locals dress up as the Grenadiers and, after a search that lasts most of the Spring Bank Holiday weekend, they stage a capture of the Earl of Rone. They then mount him backwards on a donkey to travel back to the village. He is accompanied by a Fool and a Hobby-horse who are on hand to revive him when he is repeatedly 'shot' by the guards, until finally he reaches the sea where he is summarily thrown in.

Whatever the truth behind the story, the locals managed to get the custom banned in 1837 for spending rather more time hunting for the Earl in the local pubs than maybe they should, with the entire parade descending into drunken disorderly behaviour.

Children and Families

Accents and dialects are very commonly picked up during our youth and, although in modern times we may move 'up-country' and make efforts to dilute the traces of our roots, it is all too easy to slip back into comfortable old habits as soon as we cross familiar county lines.

Access to a common language can be a tremendous asset, giving an insight into a wealth of wonderful tales from the past. Courting, for instance, has a rare amount of traditions and customs associated with it in Devon, from catching a

Wedding group

bride with a rope of flowers to shopping around for a partner at the annual fair. One farmer, when spotting a young labourer hurrying down the lane, asked:

"Where be you going with the lantern, John?"

"Going courtin', maister."

"What do 'ee want a lantern vor?"

"To zee what I be doin', maister."

"Tut, man, I never took a lantern when I went a-courtin'."

"That is what I thought, maister, when I fust zeed the missis."

He may have come off worse in this exchange, but farmers traditionally had a clear idea of their status. Out of doors, he was supreme, but in the house he fell into his place, deferring to the 'missus' on all matters domestic.

In a beautiful old poem, written by a J Marriott, a rector from Broadclyst near Exeter, the most important qualities of a marriage were likened to Devonshire's beautiful lanes. This is just an excerpt:

In a Devonshire lane, as I trotted along
T'other day, much in want of a subject for song,
Thinks I to myself, I have hit on a strain;
Sure marriage is much like a Devonshire lane.

In the first place 'tis long, and once you are in it,
It holds you so fast as a cage does a linnet;
For howe'er rough and dirty the road may be found,
Drive forward you must for there's no turning round.

But though 'tis so long, it is not very wide;
For two are the most that together can ride;
And e'en then, 'tis a chance but they get in a pother,
And jostle and cross and run foul of each other.

Then the banks are so high, to the left hand and right,

One of Devon's village lanes

That they shut up the beauties around them from sight;
And hence you'll allow 'tis an inference plain,
That marriage is just like a Devonshire lane.

Then long be the journey and narrow the way,
I'll rejoice that I've seldom a turnpike to pay;
And what e'er others say, be the last to complain
Though marriage is just like a Devonshire lane.

Schoolchildren have their own less sophisticated riddles
and rhymes, which are often drawn from the local tongue.
Many may well derive from rhymes sung throughout the
country, but it is likely that they will have been given a
particular local slant. For instance, Humpty Dumpty may
be familiar to many of us, but to a Devonshire child, he
answers to a slightly different name.

Humpitty-dumpitty
Zot 'pon a wall,
Humpitty-dumpitty
'Ad a gert vall.
An' all tha doctors in the lan'
Cudden make Humpitty-dumpitty stan'.

A child helping with the apple harvest

Being an agricultural county, many Devonian children would have spent time away from the schoolroom and working with their families on the land. It is hard to imagine the following rhyme having much place in the staid Victorian classroom, although it may have helped pass the hours of haymaking or crop picking. It has however, made it onto Facebook, just proving that some things do find an audience eventually:

A is for apple, *red as a rawse*

B is for bull, *with a ring thru eese nawse*

C is for cow, *won't do'e no 'arm*

D is for dumplin', *down on th' varm*

E is for evenin', *at the end o' th' day*

F - that's for frolics, *with th' maids in th' 'ay*

G is for granfer, *with 'ees old bandy laigs*

H is for 'ens, *layin' their aigs (eggs)*

I is for ivy, *round th'old cottage door*

J is for junket, *do'e want any more*

K is for kitchen, *where us kapes all th' grub*

L is for landlord, *at th' old village pub*

M is for moon, *th' real 'arvest sort*

N is for nuthin, *that doant cost 'e nort*

O is for 'osses, *worrited by flies*

P is for pigs, *lyin' down in their sties*

Q is for quaint, *a westcountry vew*

R is for rawses, *all covered with dew*

S is for scrumpy, *th' Devon man's liquor*

T is for tractor, *does th' job so much quicker*

U is for useless, *that's what they call Garge (George)*

V is for varmer, *th' 'ead chap in charge*

W is for Widecombe, *down on th' moor*

X is for somethin, *but I doant knaw what vor*

Y is for yokel, *a chap on th' land*

Z is zummer, *when th' countryside's grand.*

Schooling itself brought with it a change in the local culture, which the farming community had to be convinced to trust. In a series of columns in the local paper, the *Hartland Chronicle*, R Pearse Chope recorded what he called the 'Notes of the Past' between 1899 and around 1930. Among these are gems from his own childhood. For instance, when he finished school, one of his father's farm labourers said to him:

"Yu've a-bin zo long to schule that I shud think there id'n nort that yu don't knaw."

When Chope admitted there were maybe one or two things still left to learn, the response he got was unequivocal.

"Well, I zirn 'tiz a pity your father did'n bring 'e up to work. I reckon you ban't fit vor nort now - 'cept a paa'son."

Then, as now, many playground games got off to a start by means of a sorting song. Almost always ending with a line equivalent to 'you're out' these songs are as old as the hills and many variants can be found across the country. In Devon and across the west country, this version became one of the most prevalent:

Ena, mena, mona, mite;
Caska, lena, lona, lite,
Elga, belga, bo!
Eggs, butter, cheese, bread!
Stick, stock, stone dead!
O-U-T – out!

Donkey delivering to school

Last but not least is a local riddle, collected once more by Chope for one of his regular columns. Extra Devonshire expert points should be awarded if you can both translate it and guess what the subject of the riddle is:

> *Two lookers, two crookers,*
> *Vower stiff standers,*
> *Vower lily hangers,*
> *An' a whipabout.*

Farming, Industry and the Landscape

Farming has played an important role in Devon's economy for generations. The county's landscape is generally hilly and even today has a comparatively low population density, reflecting the dispersed nature of the farming communities. Many of the farms have always been run as diverse ventures, combining some crop growth with animal husbandry, cider making and a variety of other specialisms.

Many of the anecdotes which illustrate the local dialect best come from the farms, perhaps because they have excellent traditions of passing tales and legends from one generation to another, particularly when the subject can raise a smile.

Farmer with corn

One travelling curate, for instance, noted that his congregation was small and gave particular thought to the cause in his prayers:

"Us be grieved to vine that zo many o'thy vlock be he'd by on a baid o'ziekness, an be ouahle tu kom to thy tabernacle to-day; bub us be comforted by the belief that most o'm 'ull be able tu attaind to their farmerin' tomorra, an' by the assurance that they'll all be well enoo to go tu Bidevord market a Toosday."

The farming community is also infused with a wealth of traditions and customs. One that has stood the test of time and is still in evidence throughout the south-west is wassailing.

The event can be marked either on Christmas Eve or twelfth night, depending on the area, but the traditions and intent tend to be similar throughout.

A community celebration begins with a parade through the orchards, culminating with pouring large quantities of cider onto the roots of an apple tree, while singing:

Yer's tu thee, old apple tree
Be zure yu buf, be zure yu blaw,
And bring voth apples gude enough

Hats vul! Caps vul!
Dree-bushel bags vul
Pockets vul and awl!
Hurrah, hurrah!
Aw 'ess, hats vul, caps vul,
And dree-bushel bags vul.
Hurrah, hurrah!

Apple girls

Some stories are rooted less in local customs and more in the aptitudes of the farmers themselves. One story tells of a farm hand, loading corn onto a wagon. On realising he had no ladder to get down he shouted down to the farmer:

"*Her I be, sure enough, maister, but how be I to get down?*"
The farmer replied:
"*Oh, if thee shuts thee eyes and walks about a bit thee'll*
come down vast enough."

Without doubt he found a way down, as, in common with many rural communities, Devon's farmers are well known for making the most from the resources at hand. Some extreme cases have been recorded in verse:

Old Harry Trewin
Had no brutches to wear,
So he stawl a ram's skin
Vur to make en a pair;
Wi the wooly zide out
And the fleshy zide in,
They sticked pretty tight
To old Harry Trewin

The county of Devon is well served for beautiful rivers, which have inspired poets as well as being the life blood of the communities that live nearby. They are fed by weather which is changeable, particularly up on the moors where travellers have often been advised to take care. Like much of Britain, the weather is influenced by the Atlantic and the moisture that builds up in the air over the mid-Atlantic Drift comes first to the south-west.

A local poem warns of the risks the unwary take with Devon's unique weather:

Vust 'er rained,
Thin 'er bloared,
Thin 'er ailed
Thin 'er snoard;
Thin 'er cumd
A shoar o'rain;
Thin 'er vroz
An bloard agin.

The local legends did however, provide some clues as to what you might expect if you did venture out:

Mist vrom the say
Bring'th yore a dry day.
Mist vrom the 'ills
Bring'th watter to the mills.

In a county which is governed by the vagiaries of the weather, be it on the sea, moors or lowland farms, such advice should certainly be taken seriously. Nowhere is this more important than for workers in one of the regions many mines, where flooding was a constant risk.

Devon was once well known for the productivity of its mines, with rich seams of tin and copper as well as zinc, arsenic, silver and others. Some mines descended deep underground, while others concentrated their efforts in sluicing out materials that collected in stream beds and banks over millennia.

Tin mining towns were granted particular administrative rights and privileges by the crown and Devon still has four 'stannary towns': Tavistock, Ashburton, Changford and Plympton. The stannaries of Devon were so significant that they had their own laws and parliament, held in the open air at Crockern Tor, and could apply their own justice to anyone involved in the tin mining industry.

The miners developed their own language and local terminology for the tools and tricks of their trade. In Devonshire, these were recorded in The Mining Almanack of 1849, written by Henry English. It included terms such as '*attle*' referring to the rubbish heap of spent material, '*buddling*' meaning using a cistern of water used to separate ores from earth, '*streamers*' or the men who worked eroding the sides of streams to uncover hidden deposits of ore, or '*zawn*' which was a cavern underground.

One other enduring legend related to mining are the tinners rabbits. This symbol shows three hares in profile, chasing each other in a circle. Although you can find a similar image in many locations around the world, they are particularly prevalent on Dartmoor, the heart of Devon's mining country. It is likely that the miners adopted the hares symbol as their motif rather than inventing it, but it is also a clear indication of how ancient both the mythology of the hare and the occupation of mining is to the area.

Tweed Mill

Another trade to develop its own language was the weaving and cloth trade for which Devon was famous. At one time, eight out of ten Exeter residents were associated with the cloth trade, drawing upon the resources of the sheep farmers and skills of the home weavers across the county. It was only the coming of the large factories in the north and the midlands that reduced the craft to almost nothing, with very few home weavers recorded as working by the 1830s.

Specialists in textile crafts did remain though, and when Mabel Foster Bainbridge made a 'Lacemakers Pilgrimage to Devon' in 1921 she made note both of the exceptional quality and detail of the work as well as of some of the local terminology she came across:

> *"Everything abbreviated, the pillow was always 'pill,' open work 'op' and pronouns always reversed. She would ask me 'If her was goin' to bring he pill this op?' which is to say 'Did I care to come for a lesson this afternoon?'*

Making a complete study of the intricacies of local lore is made far more complicated by the myriad of different names that can be given to similar things. Nowhere is this more true than in relation to plants and animals.

In an attempt to make a study of herb lore, one collector working in Devon was examining the local varieties of wild geranium, which an elderly resident was happy to describe for him:

> *"Us calls that arb-rabbit. The oal people gathers it an' lays 'en up vor winter, to make arb tea."*

Fishermen

Fishing, Smuggling and the Sea

Devon has two long tracts of spectacular coastline, dotted along its length by small communities, isolated beaches and rugged coves. While these are now likely to be frequented most commonly by tourists, in the past they have been a hive of thriving industry.

When Daniel Defoe was touring Great Britain in the 1700s, he passed through Dartmouth, taking a trip into the harbour with some local fishermen. While out, they spotted some fish skipping on the surface of the water, which set in train a great deal of excitement:

"...*immediately one of the rowers or seamen starts up in the boat, and throwing his arms abroad, as if he had been betwitch'd, cryes out as loud as he could baul, 'a scool, a scool.' The word was taken to the shore as hastily as it would have been on land if he had cry'd fire; and by that time we reach'd the keys, the town was all in a kind of an uproar.*

In short, nobody was ready for them, except a small fishing boat, or two; one of which went out into the middle of the harbour, and at two or three hawls, took about forty thousand of them."

Like many communities that rely on the water, Devon has developed some of its own unique designs of fishing boat. The picarooner was developed in Clovelly in a style specifically suited to responding to exactly the kind of rapid call to action that Defoe recorded. It was smaller and more agile than the larger craft, meaning its crew could have it launched and on the way to a school of fish before the larger boats left shore.

The Brixham trawler was a much larger boat and pioneer of beam trawling in the late Victorian era. Being able to access the deep sea fish stocks transformed the fortunes of the south Devon fishermen and revived their flagging industry. Only six Brixham trawlers remain today, making up the Brixham heritage fleet.

Brixham trawlers

Although fishing itself has declined, some of the fishing community may have found alternative uses for their maritime heritage. A passenger ferry still runs across Teignmouth harbour, and although a short crossing, it takes some skill to negotiate the strong tides and changing weather conditions.

But the price is not something to be trifled with, as the pilot may well point out:

> *"We-e-ell, yu know – us don't charge ee nothing for the seat what you'm a-settin on; us don't charge ee nothing for them steps what you got into the boat by…"*

Teignmouth harbour

There have always been alternative uses for the skills of the fishermen, with one of the most notorious being smuggling. The extent of this trade is extremely hard to quantify as the corruption of officials was almost as notorious as the deeds of the smugglers themselves.

What is certain is that the coastline of Devon offered the perfect circumstances for smuggling to flourish: plenty of small coves and harbours, a host of isolated farms and cottages to store contraband and a wealth of experienced seamen. One centre for the illicit trade was Beer, on the south Devon coast which has been made most notorious perhaps because one of its residents, Jack Rattenbury, committed the stories of his exploits as a smuggler to paper in his 'Memoirs of a smuggler' published in 1837. In just a very short excerpt, he makes it clear that it was not an easy or altogether rewarding trade:

"I again embarked on a voyage to Cherburg, and returned with a cargo of spirits, half of which was sunk, and lost; the remainder was landed and concealed among the cliffs for three days and nights, and at last conveyed away by daylight.

I made my next and last voyage to Cherburg in the month of October in the same year, and on my return sent a man on shore to procure assistance, but he was unfortunately taken by some of the preventive men; I therefore sunk the kegs myself, but lost the whole in consequence of being laid up with a fit of the gout."

In reality, smuggling may not have been as prevalent in the south-west as the south-east, as the crossing to the continent was so much longer. The opportunity for the sea to provide a second income was still there, however, as the legends surrounding the dangerous occupation of wrecking. Customs men would often be first onto the scene of a ship foundering off the coast, but were likely to be hugely outnumbered by local villagers keen to see what washed up. There could be great loss of life, but also vast quantities of cargo, timber and supplies to be looted. The customs men may be keen to levy duties on the goods taken from the shore, while the locals were more intent on cargo getting lost, unnoticed, in the chaos.

Some histories recount tales of ships deliberately attracted onto the rocky shores, with crewmen drowned so they didn't tell tales of the lights that beckoned them in. How many lost ships can be attributed to wrecking can't fully be quantified, but the legends prevail across many seaside communities.

Nathan Hogg, a pseudonym for Henry Baird, who wrote many poems and fictional letters in the Devonshire dialect during the 19th century, wrote one poem that gives an insight into a sailors pleasure at coming home:

I zeed a zayler, tal an blithe,
Apin tha platvorm stan ;
Ha'd vetch'd thic happy time a live
Uv nether cheel nur man.

I ax'd en ware thit he wiz gwayn,
An ware ha hayl'd vrom?
Ha zed ha'd crass'd tha wat'ry mayn,
An now wiz gwayn hom.

Plymouth fish quay

Culture, Belief and Religion

It would be no surprise to learn that the parsons of Devonshire were as rooted in their rural communities as their parishioners. In one instance, a notice was posted to say that *'There will be no service held in thes church next Sunday as there is a hen sitting in the pulpit and I do not want her disturbed.'*

Men of the cloth were known for having a great respect for their agricultural flocks, and were likely to choose their wives from within the local community rather than marrying a lady from the local gentry as, given their social standing, they may otherwise have done. When asked why, one local rector declared that he was making his choices for the good of his health as well as his happiness:

"Why, man alive, due zim I want'th tu dye avore mi time?"

With further pressing he explained:

"Why, if I'd a-married a vine-vengered lady, her mid 'ave a-zend tha game tu table in a most unstomickable fashion."

Church group

Paying due consideration to the church pays dividends in Devon, as it has a rich vein of myths associated with the devil. Dartmoor particularly has a plethora of legends, starting with a dark rider hunting the moors with his pack of huge black Wisht hounds and running all the way through to the Devil's Frying Pan on Great Mis Tor where the devil is said to fry the souls of the sinners who have been sent to hell.

It also pays to attend church regularly, just in case you fall foul of the local justice system. Chope recorded in 1899 that the Hartland church housed the village stocks and as part of a penance a delinquent could be asked to come to morning prayers to apologise publicly to the congregation, before spending the rest of the day in the stocks before being released at evening prayer. The church records make note, however, of the cost of feeding those spending all day in the stocks, so vagrants who spoke nicely to a parson may find themselves a loaf of bread better off.

Some parsons may not have commanded quite so much local favour though. In one conversation, one pair of locals consider the relative benefits of the changing of personnel at the church:

"Have'ee heard the news, Jim?"
"Good or bad?"

"Bad as toothache."
"What is it?"
"Our passen's going to leave."
"I can tell 'ee worse'n that."
"Sure?"
"Eeth."
"What be'n?"
"Another passen's coming."

In some cases their lack of respect may have had some basis in reality. One rector used to invite all of the local farmers to a tithe dinner, marking the time of year farmers paid their dues to the church. He gave each of them two glasses of gin and water and while the first was drunk, he would chat with them politely. Leaving them to their own devices for the second glass, he also left them to their gossip. One farmer notes that as soon as the parson was out of earshot, they all began to abuse not just him, but the parsons throughout the county:

'They be a d-xxxx (a word too unpleasant even for history to record) grasping, skinflint set, and wrings a tenth ov everything out o' us now an' by Gor, ef us dawnt luke shaarp they'll zune 'ave a twentieth!'

Sometimes, the faith may have found itself in conflict with the local dialect, to even further comic effect. A story is told of a local man who went into a drapers shop.

"Plaize zur, I've a-vurgot whot mussus zend me vur, but tez whot they cals tha devil besides the devil."

The shopkeeper, taken aback, replied:

"How dare you allude to me and my goods as having anything to do with Satan?"

Delighted, the old man replied:

"Aw 'ess, zut, that's it, that's it! Satten! A yard-an-dree quarters ov black satten, at dree-an-sixpence a yard, an' missus zeth yu must cut et 'pon tha crass."

However, when all is said and done, the people of Devonshire did pay their respect in their own way. This prayer was recorded by Sarah Hewett as heard often among farm labourers in Dawlish and Teignmouth:

Mathew, Mark, Luke and John
Gob bless tha beyd that I lies on.
Vower cornders tu my beyd
Vower angels lie aspreyed.
Tut u vute and tut u heyd
An vower tu car me when I'm deyd.

An when I'm deyd an in m' grave
An all my boans be ratten,
Tha greedy wurms my vlaish will ayte
An I chell be vurgotten.

Bibliography

Many writers have spent time searching out examples of dialect, both in Devon and across the country. Those listed below have been tremendously valuable in the compilation of this book.

AUTHOR UNKNOWN, *An Exmoor Scolding*, in the propriety and decency of Exmoor language

AUTHOR UNKNOWN, *Fabellae Mostellariae*, Devonshire Stories in Verse (Hamilton, Adams and Company 1878)

BAINBRIDGE, M. F., *A lace makers pilgrimage to Devon* (Needle and Bobbin Club 1957)

BAIRD, H., *A new series of poems in the Devonshire dialect* (Smith 1866)

BARING-GOULD, S., *Songs of the West*, Folk Songs of Devon and Cornwall (Methuen 1905)

COXHEAD, J. R. W., *Old Devon Customs* (Raleigh Press 1957)

CROSSING, W., *Tales of the Dartmoor Pixies* (Graham 1968)

DEFOE, D., *A tour through the whole island of Great Britain* (1727)

DICKSON, A., *Devon Byways* (Westaway 1950)

ENGLISH, H., *The Mining Almanack for 1849*
(Mining Journal 1849)

FRIEND, REV H., *Bygone Devon* (Andrews and Co, 1898)

GROSE, F., *A Glossary of Provincial and Local Words Used in England* (John Russell Smith 1889)

HARRIS, J. H., *My Devonshire Book*
(Western Morning News 1907)

WORTH, R.N., *The West Country Garland*, selected works of the poets of Devon and Cornwall (1875)

The Hartland Forum website:
www.hartlandforum.co.uk